Mastering Macronutrients

A Guide to Optimal Nutrition

Stephanie Mitchell

© Copyright 2023 - All rights reserved.

Unauthorized reproduction, duplication, or transmission of this book's content is strictly prohibited without explicit consent from the author or the publisher.

Neither the publisher nor the author shall be liable for any financial loss, damages, or claims arising from the content of this book, whether directly or indirectly.

Legal Notice

This book is protected by copyright. It's intended solely for personal use. Without prior permission from the author or publisher, modifying, distributing, selling, quoting, or paraphrasing any portion of this book is forbidden.

Disclaimer Notice

The information within this document is designed for educational and entertainment purposes. All measures have been taken to ensure its accuracy and reliability. However, it comes without any implied guarantees. The author doesn't offer legal, financial, medical, or any professional counsel. Please cross-reference with other reliable sources and seek expert advice before implementing any strategies discussed herein.

Upon accessing this material, the reader acknowledges that the author won't be held accountable for any adverse outcomes, be it due to errors, omissions, or discrepancies in the content.

Contents

Introduction 1
    Why Understanding Macronutrients Matters 1

Macronutrients 101 3
    Definition and Role of Macronutrients 3
    Why Macronutrients Are Essential 4
    The Macronutrient Balance 5

Carbohydrates 7
    Carbohydrates Explained 7
    Balancing Carbohydrates in Your Diet 8

Proteins 10
    The Power of Protein 10
    Sources of Protein 11
    Protein and Muscle Health 12
    Finding Your Protein Balance 12

Fats 14

Understanding Dietary Fats 14

Healthy vs. Unhealthy Fats 15

The Role of Fats in Overall Health 16

Striking the Right Fat Balance 16

Alcohol 18

Unmasking the Hidden Calories 18

Alcohol's Impact on Macronutrients 19

Nutritional Implications of Excessive Drinking 19

Strategies for Mindful Alcohol Consumption 20

The Aftermath 21

Calories and Energy Balance 22

The Basics of Calories 22

Energy Expenditure 22

How Macronutrients Contribute to Energy 23

Achieving a Healthy Energy Balance 23

Macronutrients and Weight Management 25

Macronutrients and Weight Loss 25

Macronutrients and Weight Gain 26

Maintaining a Healthy Weight with Macronutrients 26

Finding Your Ideal Balance 26

Balanced Nutrition 28

The Importance of Balance 28

Contents

Crafting Balanced Meals 28

Portion Control 29

Meal Planning for Balanced Nutrition 30

Macronutrients for Athletes 31

Fueling Athletic Performance 31

Protein for Muscle Recovery 31

Carbohydrates for Endurance 32

Special Considerations for Athletes 32

Macronutrients and Special Diets 34

Macronutrient Considerations for Special Diets 34

Keto, Vegan, Paleo, and More 34

Customizing Macronutrients for Your Diet 35

Reading Nutrition Labels 37

Deciphering Food Labels: Unlocking the Secrets to Informed Eating 37

The Anatomy of a Nutrition Label 37

Making Informed Food Choices: A Step-by-Step Guide 39

Label Reading Tips 40

Cooking and Meal Planning 42

Building Balanced Meals from Scratch: Your Culinary Journey . 42

Balanced Meals: The Foundation of Health 42

Healthy Cooking Techniques 43

Meal Prepping for Success: Your Time-Saving Secret 44

Mindful Eating 45

The Art of Mindful Eating: A Holistic Approach 45

Strategies for Mindful Meals 46

Mindfully Controlling Macronutrient Intake 47

Building Healthy Eating Habits: A Lifelong Journey 47

Nourishing Your Health - A 40-Year-Old's Guide to Macronutrients 49

Macronutrients and Health Conditions 49

Impact of Macronutrients on Diabetes 49

Heart Health and Macronutrients 50

Other Health Considerations 51

Unmasking the Truth - Myths and Misconceptions about Macronutrients 52

Common Myths about Macronutrients 52

Debunking Nutrition Misconceptions 53

Evidence-Based Nutrition 54

Creating a Personalized Macronutrient Plan 59

Assessing Your Individual Needs 59

Setting Macronutrient Goals 60

Adjusting for Goals and Lifestyles 61

Seeking Professional Guidance 62

Recipes and Meal Ideas 64

Introduction: Healthy Eating Doesn't Mean Bland Food 64

Contents

    Breakfast 65

    Lunch 72

    Dinner 77

    Snacks 88

    Desserts 94

Supplements and Macronutrients 102

    Role of Supplements in Meeting Macronutrient Goals 102

    Considerations for Macronutrient Supplements 104

    Safety and Quality of Supplements 105

    Supplementing Wisely 105

Tracking Macronutrients 107

    Using Apps and Tools for Tracking 107

    Benefits of Keeping a Macronutrient Diary 108

    Tracking Your Progress 109

    Staying Consistent with Tracking 109

Common Challenges and Solutions 112

    Addressing Common Challenges in Macronutrient Management
    112

    Overcoming Plateaus 113

    Handling Social and Environmental Pressures 114

    Staying Committed to Your Nutritional Goals 114

Achieving Long-Term Nutritional Success 116

    Sustainable Nutrition Practices 116

Maintaining a Healthy Macronutrient Balance 117

Tips for Long-Term Nutritional Wellness 118

Your Journey to Nutritional Mastery 119

Embrace Nutritional Mastery for a Lifetime of Wellness **121**

Recap of Key Takeaways 121

Encouragement for Continued Nutritional Success 122

Glossary **124**

Introduction

Welcome to "Mastering Macronutrients: A Guide to Optimal Nutrition." As I stand here at the crossroads of my forties, I can't help but reflect on my journey through the ever-evolving landscape of health and wellness. It's a path marked by both triumphs and challenges, a journey that has taught me the incredible importance of what we put into our bodies.

In this book, we embark on a quest to decipher the secrets of macronutrients – those fundamental components of our diet that fuel our every move and shape our well-being. As a 4o-year-old woman who has experienced the ebbs and flows of life, I understand the significance of this knowledge now more than ever.

Why Understanding Macronutrients Matters

You might wonder why delving into the intricacies of macronutrients matters, especially as we navigate the busy waters of our 40s. Well, let me assure you, it matters immensely.

Our forties are a time of transformation, physically and mentally. Our bodies shift, metabolism slows, and we begin to appreciate the true value of health. It's a decade of juggling work, family, and self-care, all while trying to maintain the vitality that keeps us going.

Macronutrients – those carbohydrates, proteins, and fats that make up our daily diet – are the linchpin of this vitality. They influence our energy levels, our body composition, and our overall well-being. They have the power to sharpen our mental focus, strengthen our bodies, and even ward off the ailments that often creep in as we age.

Understanding macronutrients becomes essential because it empowers us. It gives us the knowledge to make informed choices about what we eat and how we nourish our bodies. It helps us embrace this pivotal decade with confidence, knowing that we have the tools to fuel our bodies optimally and maintain our health.

So, whether you're in your forties like me or at any stage of life, join me on this journey to unravel the mysteries of macronutrients. Together, we'll discover the transformative power of balanced nutrition, equipping ourselves with the tools to make the most of every day.

Macronutrients 101

As I enter my forties, one thing has become abundantly clear: life doesn't come with a pause button. The relentless pace of work, family, and personal growth can be both exhilarating and overwhelming. Amidst this whirlwind, I've realized that nourishing our bodies isn't just about satisfying hunger; it's about sustaining the vitality that carries us through these dynamic years. That's where macronutrients come into play.

Definition and Role of Macronutrients

Macronutrients are the superheroes of our dietary world – the proteins, carbohydrates, and fats that fuel our bodies' daily adventures. These essential nutrients serve as the building blocks of our meals, providing the energy and raw materials required for life's constant demands.

Proteins: Think of proteins as the architects of your body's structures. They're the muscle builders, the repair crew for cells, and the defenders of your immune system. They're the lean steak on your plate, the beans in your salad, and the eggs you scramble in the morning.

Carbohydrates: Carbs are your body's preferred source of energy – the fuel that propels you through your busy days. They're the grains that fill your bread, the vegetables on your plate, and the sugars that power your brain.

Fats: Fats often get a bad rap, but they're crucial for health. They're the insulators that keep your body warm, the messengers that transmit vital signals, and the storerooms for energy. You'll find them in the avocados you slice, the olive oil you drizzle, and the nuts you snack on.

Why Macronutrients Are Essential

So, why should we care about these macronutrients? Well, picture this: life as a grand performance, with each day bringing its own set of challenges and triumphs. Macronutrients are the backstage crew making it all possible.

Energy for the Journey: Carbohydrates, proteins, and fats are the power sources that keep our engines running. They provide the energy to rise with the sun, power through work meetings, and savor precious family moments.

Builders of Life: Proteins, in particular, are the architects of our very existence. They construct and repair our tissues, from the muscles that propel us forward to the antibodies that shield us from illness.

Mental Clarity and Emotional Balance: Our brains are voracious consumers of energy, relying heavily on carbohydrates to stay sharp. Balancing our macronutrients ensures that we have the mental clarity to tackle complex challenges and maintain emotional equilibrium.

The Macronutrient Balance

Achieving the right balance of macronutrients is the key to nourishing our bodies effectively. It's akin to orchestrating a symphony, where each instrument plays its part harmoniously.

But here's the catch: There's no one-size-fits-all score. Our bodies, like the seasons, change over time. In our forties, the tempo may shift, and our nutritional needs evolve. It's a dance of adaptation and understanding, a dynamic process that allows us to fine-tune our nutrition for the life we lead today.

In this book, we'll explore the intricacies of macronutrients, delve into the art of balance, and equip ourselves with the knowledge to fuel our bodies optimally. As we embrace the transformative potential of balanced nutrition, we'll find that the forties can be a remarkable chapter in the symphony of life – one where we take center stage, nourished and energized by the macronutrients that sustain our vitality.

Carbohydrates

Welcome to the captivating world of carbohydrates, where energy and flavor unite in a delightful symphony of sustenance. As we embark on our journey through our forties, understanding the intricate role of carbohydrates in our lives becomes paramount. In this chapter, we'll navigate the diverse landscape of carbs, from their essence to making wise choices that nurture our well-being.

Carbohydrates Explained

Carbohydrates are like the vibrant hues on the canvas of life, painting our days with energy, vitality, and flavor. At their core, carbohydrates are organic compounds, composed of carbon, hydrogen, and oxygen – a robust source of energy.

Simple vs. Complex Carbs: Carbohydrates come in two primary forms – simple and complex. Simple carbs are like the quick flicker of a candle, offering immediate energy. They're found in foods like candies and sugary drinks. Complex carbs, on the other hand, are the steady, dependable source of fuel. They're abundant in foods like whole grains, legumes, and vegetables.

Choosing Healthy Carbohydrate Sources: Our forties are a time when we make informed choices about our nutrition. Whole grains, such as quinoa and brown rice, become our allies, offering enduring energy and essential nutrients. Fruits and vegetables emerge as carbohydrate powerhouses, providing vitamins, minerals, and fiber alongside their natural sugars.

Balancing Carbohydrates in Your Diet

Achieving equilibrium in our carbohydrate consumption is the key to sustaining consistent energy levels. Carbs are essential in our forties when life's demands require steady fuel, but moderation is key.

Energy for Daily Life: Carbohydrates are the primary source of energy for our bodies. Balancing their intake ensures we have the endurance needed to navigate our hectic schedules.

Whole Foods and Fiber: Choosing whole, unprocessed carbohydrate sources ensures that we not only receive energy but also valuable nutrients and fiber. These keep us fuller for longer and maintain our digestive health.

In the grand symphony of our forties, carbohydrates serve as the vivacious melodies, propelling us forward with vibrant energy. They are the fuel for our daily routines, providing the strength to tackle work, family, and personal growth.

As we continue our exploration of macronutrients, we'll unravel the art of harmonizing carbohydrates with proteins and fats to craft meals that nourish our bodies and sustain our spirits throughout this dynamic decade of life.

Proteins

In the grand performance of our forties, proteins take the stage as the unsung heroes, guiding us through the intricate dance of life. As we explore this chapter, we'll discover the profound impact of proteins, the various sources available, and how they play a pivotal role in preserving our muscle health.

The Power of Protein

Proteins are the sturdy pillars that uphold the structure of our bodies, the diligent messengers that conduct essential tasks, and the fuel that drives us forward into the vibrant decade of our forties.

Building Blocks of Life: At their core, proteins are made up of amino acids, akin to the bricks that form the foundation of a sturdy house. These amino acids are the architects of our tissues, responsible for constructing and mending everything from lean muscles to the enzymes orchestrating crucial chemical reactions.

Muscle Mastery: In our forties, the importance of maintaining muscle mass cannot be overstated. It's not just about aesthetics; it's about functional strength, metabolic health, and vitality. Protein is the key player in preserving, building and repairing these vital muscles.

Sources of Protein

As we navigate the maze of life in our forties, knowing where to find high-quality sources of protein becomes paramount.

Lean Meats: Poultry, lean cuts of beef, pork, and wild game are excellent sources of protein that don't bring along excessive fat, making them perfect choices for our forties.

Plant-Based Alternatives: For those embracing a plant-based lifestyle, legumes like lentils and chickpeas, tofu, tempeh, and edamame offer ample protein.

Dairy and Eggs: Greek yogurt, cottage cheese, and eggs provide versatile and protein-rich options to diversify our diet.

Protein and Muscle Health

In our forties, maintaining muscle health is akin to preserving our vitality. Protein plays an indispensable role in this endeavor.

Muscle Construction: Adequate protein intake supports muscle growth, repair, and maintenance. Combined with targeted strength training exercises, protein-rich meals become our allies in retaining strength and mobility.

Recovery and Resilience: As we gracefully age, our bodies take a bit more time to recover from physical exertion. Protein acts as a soothing balm, reducing muscle soreness and enhancing overall recovery, ensuring we maintain the agility required for our bustling lives.

Finding Your Protein Balance

Balancing protein consumption is an art form that evolves as we progress through our forties.

Energy for Action: Protein fuels our bodies, ensuring we have the stamina to conquer daily challenges. It becomes the cornerstone of our nutrition, empowering us to face our busy schedules head-on.

Whole Foods and Wellness: Opting for whole, unprocessed protein sources ensures we receive not only energy but also essential nutrients and dietary fiber. These elements keep us full, support our digestive health, and maintain overall well-being.

As we proceed on this journey through macronutrients, we'll unravel the art of harmonizing proteins with carbohydrates and fats to craft meals that nourish our bodies and sustain our spirits throughout this dynamic decade of life.

Fats

In the grand narrative of our forties, fats emerge as both the enigmatic shadows and the guiding stars, shaping the storyline of our well-being. As we delve into this chapter, we'll embark on a journey to decipher the intricacies of dietary fats, distinguish between the virtuous and the villainous, and understand their profound influence on our overall health.

Understanding Dietary Fats

Fats are the multifaceted characters in our nutritional story, offering flavor, energy, and essential functions in our bodies. In our forties, comprehending the nuances of these fats becomes a vital skill.

The Three Musketeers: Dietary fats come in three primary forms: saturated fats, unsaturated fats, and trans fats. Each type carries a unique role and impact on our health. Saturated fats, like the steadfast guard, are generally solid at room temperature and can be found in red meat and dairy products. Unsaturated fats, the flexible troubadours, are liquid at room temperature and are prevalent in plant-based oils, nuts, and fatty fish. Trans fats, the masked infiltrators, are artificial fats often found in processed and fried foods.

Calories and Energy: Fats are calorie-dense, offering a concentrated source of energy. In our forties, they provide the staying power we need to fuel our vibrant lives. However, it's essential to tread carefully, as excessive fat consumption can lead to weight gain.

Healthy vs. Unhealthy Fats

In the evolving narrative of our forties, distinguishing between the heroes and the villains among fats is crucial.

Healthy Allies: Unsaturated fats, especially monounsaturated and polyunsaturated fats, emerge as our allies. They champion heart health, reduce inflammation, and support cognitive function. Foods like avocados, olive oil, and fatty fish become our go-to choices.

The Villains Within: Saturated and trans fats, the antagonists of our story, are known culprits in heart disease and other health issues. Limiting our intake of foods high in these fats, such as processed snacks and fried delights, becomes paramount.

The Role of Fats in Overall Health

As we take center stage in our forties, understanding how fats influence our health becomes paramount.

Heart Health: Unsaturated fats, particularly omega-3 fatty acids found in fish, play a leading role in reducing the risk of heart disease. Incorporating these fats into our diet becomes an investment in our future.

Brain and Nervous System: Fats are integral components of our brain and nervous system. They facilitate cognitive function, memory, and overall mental well-being. In our forties, these functions become more precious than ever.

Striking the Right Fat Balance

In the captivating drama of our forties, finding the perfect balance of dietary fats becomes an art.

Moderation and Variety: Moderation is our guiding principle. Balancing saturated fats with unsaturated fats while minimizing trans fats keeps our nutrition in harmony. Diversity in fat sources ensures we receive a spectrum of nutrients.

Cooking with Wisdom: Opt for cooking methods that preserve the integrity of healthy fats. Grilling, roasting, and steaming are our allies, while deep frying takes a backseat.

In our pursuit of well-being, fats are the characters that add depth and flavor to our forties. With knowledge and discernment, we embrace these elements, ensuring that our nutritional narrative remains vibrant and harmonious throughout this remarkable decade of life.

Alcohol

In this chapter, we'll take a closer look at alcohol and its impact on our nutritional balance, particularly from the perspective of a 40-year-old woman. Alcohol is often enjoyed socially, and understanding its effects on your diet and health is crucial for making informed choices.

Unmasking the Hidden Calories

Alcohol and Calories: Alcohol contains calories, and it's essential to recognize these hidden calories. For every gram of alcohol consumed, you're taking in about 7 calories. This is significant because alcohol calories often go unnoticed, and they can add up quickly.

Comparison to Macronutrients: Let's put these alcohol calories into perspective. For instance, one gram of carbohydrates also provides about 4 calories, while one gram of protein offers the same. In contrast, one gram of fat packs a whopping 9 calories. So, while alcohol isn't the most calorie-dense substance, it's still calorically significant.

Alcohol's Impact on Macronutrients

The Macronutrient Makeup of Alcohol: Beyond calories, alcohol contains other components, including carbohydrates and sugars. Some mixed drinks even have small amounts of proteins. However, alcohol itself doesn't provide any essential nutrients like vitamins or minerals. Understanding this composition is vital in comprehending how it fits into your overall macronutrient intake.

Disruption of Macronutrient Balance: Alcohol can disrupt the balance between carbohydrates, proteins, and fats in your diet. When you drink alcohol, your body prioritizes metabolizing it over other nutrients, which can interfere with your body's macronutrient utilization. Additionally, excessive alcohol consumption can lead to unhealthy eating choices, potentially skewing your macronutrient ratios.

Nutritional Implications of Excessive Drinking

Calories and Poor Food Choices: Excessive drinking often goes hand in hand with poor food choices. Alcohol can lower inhibitions and impair judgment, leading to overeating or choosing less nutritious foods. This can disrupt your nutritional goals and contribute to weight gain.

Balancing Alcohol and Nutrition: Finding a balance between enjoying alcoholic beverages and maintaining your nutritional goals is essential. It's crucial to be mindful of your alcohol consumption, particularly if you're striving for a specific macronutrient balance or weight management.

Strategies for Mindful Alcohol Consumption

Savoring the Moment: Mindful drinking involves savoring the flavors and experiences of alcoholic drinks in moderation. This approach emphasizes quality over quantity. Instead of consuming numerous drinks, consider enjoying one or two thoughtfully selected beverages.

Smart Choices: When choosing alcoholic drinks, opt for options that align with your nutritional goals. For example, select beverages that are lower in sugar and empty calories. Lighter beers, wines, or spirits with low-calorie mixers can be better choices.

The Aftermath

Recovery from Excess: If you've indulged in excessive drinking, it's essential to focus on recovery. Hydration is crucial; alcohol can dehydrate your body, so drink plenty of water. Nutrient-rich foods can help replenish essential vitamins and minerals that may have been depleted during drinking.

Moderation and Balance: The key takeaway is that moderation and balance are the pillars of responsible alcohol consumption. By understanding the caloric content of alcohol, its impact on macronutrients, and the potential consequences of excessive drinking, you can make informed choices that align with your nutritional and health goals.

In this chapter, we've demystified the connection between alcohol and nutrition. Armed with this knowledge, you can navigate social situations and enjoy alcoholic beverages mindfully while maintaining your macronutrient balance and overall well-being. Cheers to informed choices and a healthier life!

Calories and Energy Balance

The Basics of Calories

In our 40s, understanding calories becomes more crucial than ever. Calories are the energy units our bodies use for everything we do – from breathing to running marathons. Each day, we need a certain number of calories to maintain our current weight and support our activities. These calories primarily come from the foods we eat, and they come in the form of macronutrients: carbohydrates, proteins, and fats.

Energy Expenditure

As we age, our metabolism naturally starts to slow down. This means our bodies burn fewer calories at rest. However, we can't blame everything on our metabolism. Our daily activities also play a significant role in calorie expenditure. Whether it's going to work, exercising, cleaning the house, or even fidgeting, these activities contribute to our total daily energy expenditure (TDEE).

How Macronutrients Contribute to Energy

Carbohydrates, proteins, and fats are the macronutrients that make up our food. Each of them provides a different number of calories per gram. Carbohydrates and proteins offer about 4 calories per gram, while fats provide 9 calories per gram. This is essential to know because the macronutrient balance in our diet directly impacts our daily calorie intake.

Carbohydrates are our body's preferred energy source. When we consume them, they are converted into glucose, which our cells use for energy. Proteins, on the other hand, are not primarily an energy source but play a crucial role in muscle health and repair. Fats, despite their higher calorie density, are essential for overall health, including hormone production and brain function.

Achieving a Healthy Energy Balance

Maintaining a healthy energy balance is essential for us in our 40s. It's all about matching the number of calories we consume through our diet with the calories we burn through our activities. To maintain our current weight, we need to be in what's called caloric maintenance. Consuming more calories than we burn leads to weight gain while burning more calories than we consume results in weight loss.

A healthy energy balance isn't solely about restricting calories. It's also about the quality of those calories. A well-balanced diet that includes a variety of nutrient-dense foods ensures we get not only the right number of calories but also the essential vitamins and minerals needed to support overall health.

In our 4os, achieving and maintaining a healthy energy balance becomes increasingly important. It sets the foundation for our overall well-being and can help us manage weight, stay active, and enjoy life to the fullest. By understanding the basics of calories, tracking our energy expenditure, and being mindful of how macronutrients contribute to our energy intake, we can make informed dietary choices that support our health and vitality.

Macronutrients and Weight Management

Macronutrients and Weight Loss

In our 40s, many of us find that managing our weight becomes a bit more challenging than it was in our younger years. Understanding how macronutrients play a role in weight management is key to achieving and maintaining a healthy weight.

When it comes to weight loss, the focus often turns to reducing calorie intake. But it's equally important to consider the types of calories we consume. Carbohydrates, proteins, and fats all play unique roles in our bodies. Carbs provide a quick source of energy, while proteins support muscle health and repair, and fats are essential for various bodily functions. A balanced approach that includes these macronutrients can help us feel full, satisfied, and energized while reducing overall calorie intake.

Macronutrients and Weight Gain

On the flip side, weight gain can be a concern in our 40s. Some hormonal changes may slow down our metabolism, making it easier to gain weight. Macronutrients can influence weight gain differently. Carbohydrates can lead to quick spikes and crashes in blood sugar levels, potentially triggering cravings and overeating. Protein can help us feel full and maintain lean muscle mass, while dietary fats, when consumed in excess, contribute to weight gain.

Maintaining a Healthy Weight with Macronutrients

Maintaining a healthy weight as we age requires a balanced approach to macronutrients. This means choosing complex carbohydrates that provide sustained energy, incorporating lean protein sources to support muscle health, and including healthy fats like those found in avocados and nuts. It's not about excluding any macronutrient entirely but rather finding the right balance that works for our bodies.

Finding Your Ideal Balance

There's no one-size-fits-all approach when it comes to macronutrients and weight management. Our bodies are

Macronutrients and Weight Management

unique, and what works for one person may not work for another. Finding our ideal macronutrient balance involves experimentation and paying attention to how different foods make us feel.

In our 40s, it's more important than ever to focus on nourishing our bodies and supporting overall health rather than pursuing extreme diets or restrictions. By understanding how macronutrients impact our weight, we can make informed choices that help us achieve and maintain a healthy weight while feeling energized and vibrant. Remember, it's not just about the number on the scale; it's about feeling our best at every stage of life.

Balanced Nutrition

The Importance of Balance

As we reach our 40s, maintaining our health and well-being becomes increasingly important. Balanced nutrition is the cornerstone of a healthy and fulfilling life during this stage. But what exactly does balanced nutrition entail?

Balanced nutrition is about more than just what we eat; it's about how we nourish our bodies. It means finding the right mix of macronutrients – carbohydrates, proteins, and fats – along with essential vitamins and minerals. Achieving this balance is crucial for supporting our overall health, energy levels, and even our mental well-being.

Crafting Balanced Meals

Crafting balanced meals involves including a variety of foods from different food groups. Whole grains provide complex carbohydrates for sustained energy, while lean proteins support muscle health and repair. Healthy fats, like those found in avocados and olive oil, are essential for our bodies' many functions.

Balanced meals also include plenty of fruits and vegetables, which provide essential vitamins, minerals, and fiber. These components work together to create meals that not only taste good but also nourish our bodies from the inside out.

Portion Control

Portion control is another key aspect of balanced nutrition. As we age, our metabolism may slow down, making it easier to gain weight if we don't pay attention to portion sizes. It's not about depriving ourselves but rather being mindful of how much we eat.

Practicing portion control allows us to enjoy the foods we love without overindulging. It also helps prevent that uncomfortable feeling of being overly full, which can lead to digestive discomfort.

Meal Planning for Balanced Nutrition

One of the best strategies for achieving balanced nutrition is meal planning. In our busy lives, it's easy to make hasty food choices that may not support our health goals. Meal planning empowers us to make thoughtful choices and ensure that we're getting the right balance of nutrients in our diet.

By setting aside some time each week to plan our meals and snacks, we can make sure we have healthy options readily available. This reduces the temptation to grab convenience foods that might not align with our nutritional needs.

In our 40s, balanced nutrition is our ally in maintaining our health, vitality, and resilience. It's not about dieting or depriving ourselves but about making informed choices that support our overall well-being. By embracing the principles of balance, crafting nourishing meals, practicing portion control, and incorporating meal planning into our lives, we can make balanced nutrition a sustainable part of our healthy lifestyle.

Macronutrients for Athletes

Fueling Athletic Performance

When you reach your 40s, staying active becomes even more critical for your health and well-being. Whether you're a seasoned athlete or just enjoy regular exercise, understanding how macronutrients can support your physical activity is vital.

Fueling athletic performance involves providing your body with the right nutrients at the right times. Carbohydrates are your primary source of energy, especially during high-intensity workouts. Including complex carbohydrates like whole grains, fruits, and vegetables in your diet can help sustain your energy levels.

Protein for Muscle Recovery

For those of us who engage in regular physical activity, protein is essential for muscle recovery and repair. As we age, preserving muscle mass becomes increasingly important, and protein plays a pivotal role in this process.

Incorporating lean sources of protein like chicken, fish, beans, and tofu into your meals can support muscle health. Don't forget to include some protein-rich snacks post-workout to aid in recovery.

Carbohydrates for Endurance

Carbohydrates are not only essential for energy but also for endurance. If you enjoy activities like running, cycling, or swimming, you'll want to ensure you have enough carbohydrates to fuel those longer workouts.

Complex carbohydrates like oatmeal, quinoa, and sweet potatoes can sustain your energy levels during endurance exercises. Planning your carbohydrate intake around your workouts can make a noticeable difference in your performance.

Special Considerations for Athletes

As a 40-year-old woman who loves staying active, it's important to be mindful of any special dietary considerations. Hydration is critical, especially if you're sweating a lot during exercise. Water should be your go-to choice, but sports drinks with electrolytes can be helpful during particularly intense workouts.

Additionally, consider the timing of your meals in relation to your workouts. Eating a balanced meal a couple of hours before exercise can provide the necessary fuel. After your workout, a combination of protein and carbohydrates can aid in recovery.

In your 4os, staying active is an investment in your health and well-being. Understanding how macronutrients can support your athletic endeavors is a valuable tool in your wellness toolkit. By fueling your performance with the right balance of carbohydrates and protein and considering special considerations like hydration and meal timing, you can enjoy an active and fulfilling lifestyle for years to come.

Macronutrients and Special Diets

Macronutrient Considerations for Special Diets

As we enter our 40s, many of us may explore various dietary choices for health, ethical, or personal reasons. Understanding how macronutrients fit into these special diets is essential for maintaining our well-being.

Special diets, such as keto, vegan, and paleo, often have specific macronutrient requirements. It's crucial to educate ourselves about these dietary approaches and how they impact our macronutrient intake.

Keto, Vegan, Paleo, and More

The keto diet, characterized by low carbs and high fats, has gained popularity for its potential weight loss benefits. For someone in their 40s, managing weight can become more challenging, making the keto diet an appealing option.

Veganism, on the other hand, excludes all animal products. This diet requires careful planning to ensure an adequate intake of essential nutrients, particularly protein and vitamin B$_{12}$.

Paleo focuses on whole, unprocessed foods and mimics the diet of our Paleolithic ancestors. It emphasizes high-protein sources and healthy fats while limiting grains and processed foods.

Customizing Macronutrients for Your Diet

The key to success with special diets lies in customizing your macronutrients to align with your chosen approach. For example, if you're following a keto diet, you'll want to increase your healthy fat intake while drastically reducing carbs.

For vegans, it's essential to find plant-based sources of protein and ensure adequate intake. Protein-rich foods like tofu, beans, and quinoa become dietary staples.

Paleo enthusiasts can enjoy lean proteins, nuts, and seeds while minimizing grains and dairy. Balancing macronutrients within these dietary frameworks is key to reaping their benefits.

Understanding these special diets and their macronutrient nuances can help you make informed choices as you navigate your 40s. Whether you choose keto, vegan, paleo, or another approach, personalizing your macronutrient intake will support your health and well-being on your unique dietary journey.

Reading Nutrition Labels

Deciphering Food Labels: Unlocking the Secrets to Informed Eating

Welcome to a crucial chapter in your nutritional journey, where we'll delve deep into the art of reading and deciphering nutrition labels. As we navigate this landscape together, you'll gain a comprehensive understanding of how to utilize these labels effectively.

The Anatomy of a Nutrition Label

Nutrition labels are your gateway to making informed food choices. At first glance, they might appear overwhelming, but let's break down their components:

1. **Serving Size:** This is the starting point. It tells you the quantity of food the nutrition facts refer to. Pay close attention here, as many people underestimate serving sizes.

2. **Calories:** The number of calories per serving. This figure sets the stage for understanding the energy content of the food.

3. **Macronutrients:** This is where we dive deeper. The macronutrients include:

   ❖ **Total Fat:** Both the quantity (in grams) and the type (saturated and trans fats) are specified. Understanding the types of fats is crucial, as some are heart-healthy while others should be limited.

   ❖ **Cholesterol:** Given in milligrams, this value is important, especially if you need to monitor your heart health.

   ❖ **Sodium:** Listed in milligrams, it's a critical number for those watching their blood pressure.

   ❖ **Total Carbohydrates:** This section includes dietary fiber and sugars. Fiber is essential for digestive health, while added sugars should be limited.

   ❖ **Protein:** Grams of protein per serving are highlighted. Protein is vital for various bodily functions, including muscle maintenance and immune support.

4. **Vitamins and Minerals:** Some labels will show the percentage of daily recommended intake for certain vitamins and minerals.

5. **% Daily Value:** This figure indicates how much a nutrient in one serving contributes to a daily diet. It's typically based on a

daily intake of 2,000 calories, which is a standard reference point.

Making Informed Food Choices: A Step-by-Step Guide

1. Start with Serving Size: Always begin by checking the serving size. If you eat more or less than the specified serving, adjust the nutrient values accordingly.

2. Calories Count: Consider the calorie count per serving. This number sets the stage for understanding the energy the food provides.

3. Evaluate Macronutrients: Dig into the macronutrients:

- **Total Fat:** Aim for a balance between healthy fats like monounsaturated and polyunsaturated fats while limiting saturated and trans fats.

- **Cholesterol:** Keep this in check, especially if you're managing heart health.

- **Sodium:** Watch your sodium intake, especially if you have high blood pressure.

- **Total Carbohydrates:** Focus on fiber content and be mindful of added sugars.

- ❖ **Protein:** Ensure you're getting an adequate amount, especially if you're active or looking to maintain muscle mass.

4. % Daily Value: Use this as a general guide to see how a food fits into your overall daily diet. For instance, a food item with 20% or more of the daily value for a nutrient is considered high.

5. Ingredients List: Don't forget to scan the ingredients list. Ingredients are listed in descending order of quantity, so if sugars or unhealthy fats are near the top, be cautious.

Label Reading Tips

- ❖ Portion Control: Pay attention to serving sizes to avoid overeating.

- ❖ Compare Products: Use labels to compare similar products and choose the one that aligns with your dietary goals.

- ❖ Hidden Sugars and Fats: Look out for aliases of sugars (corn syrup, high fructose corn syrup) and unhealthy fats (partially hydrogenated oils).

By mastering the art of reading nutrition labels, you're not just making informed choices; you're empowering yourself to take control of your health in your 40s and beyond. It's a skill that will serve you well on your journey to optimal nutrition and well-being.

Cooking and Meal Planning

Building Balanced Meals from Scratch: Your Culinary Journey

Welcome to the heart of your nutritional transformation – cooking and meal planning. In this chapter, we'll embark on a culinary adventure, learning how to create delicious, balanced meals from scratch that nourish not just your body but also your soul.

Balanced Meals: The Foundation of Health

Creating balanced meals is an art that combines flavors, nutrients, and personal preferences. Here's how to do it:

1. **Include All Macronutrients:** A balanced meal comprises carbohydrates, proteins, and healthy fats. Aim for variety to

ensure you get a broad spectrum of nutrients.

2. **Colorful Vegetables:** Fill your plate with vibrant veggies. They're rich in vitamins, minerals, and fiber, promoting digestive health and overall well-being.

3. **Lean Proteins:** Opt for lean protein sources like lean beef, wild game, poultry, fish, beans, and tofu. Protein supports muscle health and keeps you feeling full.

4. **Whole Grains:** Choose whole grains like quinoa, brown rice, and oats for sustained energy and fiber.

5. **Healthy Fats:** Incorporate sources of healthy fats like avocados, olive oil, and nuts. They're great for heart health and satiety.

Healthy Cooking Techniques

1. **Baking:** A low-fat method that's perfect for roasting vegetables or lean proteins.

2. **Grilling:** Enhances flavors without adding extra fats.

3. **Steaming:** Preserves nutrients in vegetables.

4. **Sautéing:** Use a small amount of oil to cook quickly while retaining flavor.

5. **Stir-frying:** A quick, high-heat method for cooking lean proteins and veggies.

Meal Prepping for Success: Your Time-Saving Secret

Meal prepping is a game-changer. Here's how to make it work:

1. **Plan Ahead:** Design a weekly menu with balanced meals and snacks.

2. **Grocery Shopping:** Make a detailed shopping list to avoid impulse buys.

3. **Batch Cooking:** Prepare staples like grains, proteins, and sauces in advance.

4. **Portion Control:** Use meal prep containers to portion out meals and snacks.

5. **Variety is Key:** Keep it interesting by rotating ingredients and flavors.

By mastering the art of cooking and meal planning, you're not only nourishing your body but also embracing a healthier, more enjoyable way of eating in your 40s and beyond. It's a journey that offers both satisfaction and well-being, one delicious meal at a time.

Mindful Eating

In this chapter, we'll explore the art of mindful eating and how it can transform your relationship with food as you navigate your 40s and beyond.

The Art of Mindful Eating: A Holistic Approach

Mindful eating is more than just a trend; it's a practice that encourages you to be present and fully engaged with your food. Here's why it matters:

- **Savoring Every Bite:** Instead of rushing through meals, savor each flavor, texture, and aroma.

- **Connecting with Hunger and Fullness:** Tune into your body's hunger and fullness cues, helping you avoid overeating.

- ❖ **Reducing Emotional Eating:** Mindful eating can prevent impulsive eating triggered by stress or emotions.

- ❖ **Enjoyment and Satisfaction:** When you truly enjoy your food, you're less likely to crave unhealthy options.

Strategies for Mindful Meals

1. **Slow Down:** Take your time, chew slowly, and put your utensils down between bites. This gives your body time to register fullness.

2. **Engage Your Senses:** Pay attention to the colors, textures, and scents of your food. Engaging your senses enhances the dining experience.

3. **Limit Distractions:** Avoid eating in front of screens or while multitasking. Focus solely on your meal.

4. **Portion Control:** Use smaller plates and bowls to help control portion sizes.

5. **Express Gratitude:** Take a moment to appreciate the effort that went into preparing your meal. This can increase your enjoyment.

Mindfully Controlling Macronutrient Intake

Mindful eating can extend to macronutrients. Here's how to incorporate this practice into your diet:

- ❖ **Balanced Macros:** Ensure your meals include a balance of carbohydrates, proteins, and healthy fats.

- ❖ **Listen to Your Body:** Pay attention to how different macronutrients make you feel. Adjust your intake based on your energy needs.

- ❖ **Carbohydrate Choices:** Opt for complex carbs for sustained energy and simple carbs sparingly for quick fuel.

- ❖ **Protein for Satiety:** Include lean proteins to help you feel full and satisfied.

- ❖ **Healthy Fats:** Embrace sources of healthy fats for overall health and taste.

Building Healthy Eating Habits: A Lifelong Journey

Mindful eating isn't a diet; it's a sustainable way of approaching food. By practicing mindful eating, you can:

- ❖ **Improve Digestion:** Proper chewing aids digestion and nutrient absorption.

- ❖ **Enhance Satisfaction:** Truly enjoying your meals can reduce cravings for unhealthy foods.

- ❖ **Support Healthy Weight Management:** Mindful eating helps regulate food intake and fosters a healthier relationship with food.

- ❖ **Promote Long-Term Health:** Consistent mindfulness can lead to better overall health and well-being.

Embracing mindful eating in your 40s is a gift to yourself – a way to fully experience the pleasures of food while nourishing your body and soul. By making this practice a part of your daily life, you'll cultivate a lifelong relationship with food that brings joy and vitality.

Nourishing Your Health - A 40-Year-Old's Guide to Macronutrients

In your 40s, maintaining good health becomes increasingly important. Let's delve into the connection between macronutrients and various health conditions.

Macronutrients and Health Conditions

Macronutrients play a crucial role in our health, and their impact becomes more evident with age. Here, we'll explore how they relate to specific health conditions.

Impact of Macronutrients on Diabetes

If you or someone you know is dealing with diabetes, understanding how macronutrients affect blood sugar is essential:

- **Carbohydrates and Blood Sugar:** Learn to manage carbohydrate intake to control blood glucose levels.

- **Protein's Role:** Discover how protein can help stabilize blood sugar and support overall health.

- **Healthy Fats for Diabetics:** Understand which fats are best for diabetes management.

Heart Health and Macronutrients

Heart health is a priority at any age. Here's how macronutrients influence it:

- **Carbs and Heart Health:** Recognize the impact of different carbohydrate sources on heart health.

- **Protein for Cardiovascular Wellness:** Explore the link between protein intake and heart disease prevention.

- **Fats and Your Heart:** Understand how dietary fats can either promote or protect against heart issues.

Other Health Considerations

Beyond diabetes and heart health, macronutrients can affect various aspects of your well-being:

- ❖ **Weight and Joint Health:** Excess weight can strain joints. Learn how macronutrients can support a healthy weight.

- ❖ **Bone Health:** Calcium and vitamin D are key for maintaining strong bones. Find out how macronutrients fit in.

- ❖ **Digestive Health:** Fiber-rich carbohydrates are essential for digestion. Discover their role in gut health.

- ❖ **Skin and Hair:** Proteins support the growth and repair of skin and hair tissues.

- ❖ **Brain Health:** Healthy fats are vital for brain function. Explore their impact on cognitive well-being.

As a 40-year-old, your health journey is unique. Understanding how macronutrients interact with your body can help you make informed choices that support your overall well-being.

Unmasking the Truth - Myths and Misconceptions about Macronutrients

In this chapter, we'll uncover and systematically debunk common myths and misconceptions surrounding macronutrients, using solid evidence-based nutrition.

Common Myths about Macronutrients

Myth 1: Carbs Are the Enemy

Debunked: Carbohydrates are not the enemy. They are our body's primary source of energy. Complex carbohydrates, found in whole grains, fruits, and vegetables, provide essential nutrients and fiber. It's the overconsumption of refined and sugary carbs that can lead to health issues.

Myth 2: Protein Overload Is Ideal

Debunked: While protein is crucial for muscle repair and overall health, excessive protein intake doesn't equate to better health. The body has limits on how much protein it can utilize efficiently. Consuming excessive protein may strain the kidneys and have no added benefit for most individuals.

Myth 3: Fats Make You Fat

Debunked: Dietary fats are not solely responsible for weight gain. In fact, healthy fats like those found in avocados, nuts, and olive oil are essential for various bodily functions. Weight gain often results from consuming more calories than your body needs, regardless of the source.

Debunking Nutrition Misconceptions

Misconception 1: Skipping Meals Helps with Weight Loss

Debunked: Skipping meals can lead to overeating later in the day and can slow down your metabolism. It's more effective to have regular, balanced meals and snacks to maintain steady energy levels and control appetite.

Misconception 2: All Calories Are Equal

Debunked: Calories from different sources affect the body differently. For example, calories from whole foods with fiber and nutrients provide better satiety and nutrition than empty calories from sugary beverages.

Misconception 3: Macronutrient Ratios Are Universal

Debunked: There's no one-size-fits-all macronutrient ratio. Individual factors like age, activity level, metabolism, and health goals influence the ideal macronutrient distribution. Customization is key for a sustainable diet.

Evidence-Based Nutrition

Your Roadmap to Evidence-Based Eating

By the chapter's end, you'll have the tools to make informed nutritional decisions based on science. You'll know how to separate fact from fiction and be equipped with the knowledge to create a personalized, evidence-based eating plan tailored to your unique needs and goals.

Evaluating Nutritional Claims and Fad Diets: A Guide to Credibility

In today's information age, we're constantly bombarded with nutritional claims and fad diets promising quick fixes and miraculous results. To make informed dietary choices, it's essential to critically evaluate these claims, relying on credible sources and peer-reviewed studies. Here's a guide to help you separate fact from fiction:

1. Beware of Quick Fixes:

- ❖ **Red Flag:** Claims that sound too good to be true often are. Be skeptical of diets or products promising rapid, effortless weight loss or instant health improvements.

- ❖ **Credible Source:** Sustainable changes to diet and lifestyle, rather than quick fixes, are backed by science. Look for information promoting gradual, long-term improvements.

2. Scrutinize Anecdotal Evidence:

- ❖ **Red Flag:** Personal testimonials and anecdotes can be persuasive, but they are not scientific evidence. What works for one person may not work for another.

- ❖ **Credible Source:** Rely on peer-reviewed studies and research that involve a large and diverse sample of participants. Scientific studies provide more reliable data than individual experiences.

3. Evaluate the Credentials:

- ❖ **Red Flag:** Be cautious of sources lacking appropriate credentials or relevant expertise in nutrition and health. Anyone can claim to be an expert online.

- **Credible Source:** Trust information from registered dietitians, nutritionists, or healthcare professionals with recognized qualifications. Peer-reviewed journals are also reliable sources.

4. Check for Bias and Conflicts of Interest:

- **Red Flag:** Be wary of sources or studies funded by companies or organizations with a vested interest in promoting a specific product or diet.

- **Credible Source:** Seek out studies or information from sources with no conflicts of interest. Transparent and unbiased research is more likely to provide accurate insights.

5. Assess the Scientific Method:

- **Red Flag:** Lack of scientific rigor, small sample sizes, or poorly designed studies can lead to unreliable results.

- **Credible Source:** High-quality studies follow the scientific method, with clear research questions, methodology, and peer review. Look for studies published in reputable scientific journals.

6. Consider the Overall Consensus:

- Red Flag: A single study or a few outliers can't outweigh the consensus of scientific research.

- ❖ **Credible Source:** Assess the overall body of evidence. When the majority of studies and experts agree on a topic, it's a stronger indication of credibility.

7. Avoid Extreme Claims:

- ❖ **Red Flag:** Diets or products claiming to cure all ailments, diseases, or conditions are highly suspect.

- ❖ **Credible Source:** Understand that nutrition is complex, and no single diet or product can address all health issues. Be cautious of anything promising miraculous outcomes.

8. Question Over-Restrictive Diets:

- ❖ **Red Flag:** Diets that eliminate entire food groups or severely restrict calorie intake can be unhealthy and unsustainable.

- ❖ **Credible Source:** Opt for balanced, evidence-based diets that promote a variety of foods and sustainable eating patterns.

9. Use Reliable Fact-Checking Sites:

- ❖ **Red Flag:** Misinformation spreads easily on the internet. Don't rely solely on social media or unverified websites.

- **Credible Source:** Fact-checking websites and reputable health organizations often debunk nutritional myths and pseudoscientific claims.

10. **Consult a Professional:**

- **Credible Source:** When in doubt or when considering a significant dietary change, consult a registered dietitian or healthcare provider. They can provide personalized guidance based on your individual needs and health goals.

By applying these principles and critically assessing nutritional claims and fad diets, you'll be better equipped to make informed dietary choices grounded in credible, evidence-based information. Remember that nutrition is a complex field, and relying on scientifically validated sources is the key to achieving and maintaining a healthy diet.

Creating a Personalized Macronutrient Plan

As a 40-year-old woman, I understand the importance of maintaining a healthy and balanced diet to support my overall well-being. Creating a personalized macronutrient plan has been a game-changer on my journey toward optimal health and fitness. In this chapter, we will explore the steps to assess your individual needs, set macronutrient goals, adjust for your goals and lifestyle, and when necessary, seek professional guidance.

Assessing Your Individual Needs

Before embarking on your macronutrient journey, it's crucial to assess your individual needs. Factors such as age, gender, weight, activity level, and health goals play a significant role in determining your macronutrient requirements.

1. **Calculate Basal Metabolic Rate (BMR):** Start by calculating your BMR, the number of calories your body needs at rest. There are various online calculators and formulas available to help with this.

2. **Consider Activity Level:** Take into account your daily activity level. Are you mostly sedentary, moderately active, or highly active? This will influence your total daily calorie needs.

3. **Set Protein Requirements:** Ensure an adequate protein intake to support muscle maintenance and repair. Aim for around 0.8 to 1.2 grams of protein per pound of body weight.

4. **Determine Fat Intake:** Include healthy fats in your diet for energy and overall health. Aim for 20-35% of your total daily calories from fats, with a focus on unsaturated fats.

5. **Carbohydrate Considerations:** The remaining calories can come from carbohydrates. Adjust this based on your preference, energy needs, and dietary restrictions.

Setting Macronutrient Goals

With a better understanding of your individual needs, it's time to set specific macronutrient goals. These goals can vary based on your objectives, whether it's weight loss, muscle gain, or simply maintaining your current weight.

1. **Weight Loss:** If your goal is to lose weight, you may want to create a calorie deficit by reducing your overall calorie intake while maintaining adequate protein intake.

2. **Muscle Gain:** For those aiming to build muscle, focus on increasing your protein intake and adjusting your calorie intake to support muscle growth.

3. **Maintenance:** To maintain your current weight, ensure that your calorie intake matches your energy expenditure. Balance your macronutrients accordingly.

Adjusting for Goals and Lifestyles

Creating a personalized macronutrient plan is not a one-size-fits-all approach. It's essential to adapt your plan to your unique circumstances and lifestyle.

1. **Consider Dietary Preferences:** Tailor your macronutrient plan to accommodate your dietary preferences, whether you're vegetarian, vegan, or follow a specific eating style.

2. **Meal Timing:** Pay attention to meal timing and frequency. Some individuals thrive on frequent small meals, while others prefer intermittent fasting.

3. Track Progress: Regularly monitor your progress and make adjustments as needed. Your macronutrient needs may change over time as your body composition and fitness goals evolve.

Seeking Professional Guidance

While creating a personalized macronutrient plan can be empowering, it's essential to seek professional guidance when necessary.

1. Registered Dietitian: If you have specific health concerns, or complex dietary needs, or are unsure about creating a plan on your own, consult a registered dietitian. They can provide expert guidance tailored to your situation.

2. Fitness Coach: If your macronutrient goals are closely tied to fitness and athletic performance, consider working with a certified fitness coach who can design a comprehensive plan.

In conclusion, crafting a personalized macronutrient plan is a powerful tool on your journey to better health and well-being. By assessing your individual needs, setting clear goals, adjusting for your unique lifestyle, and seeking professional guidance when necessary, you can embark on a path toward a healthier, more balanced life.

Creating a Personalized Macronutrient Plan

"In our journey towards better health and nutrition, I want to offer you a unique opportunity. By visiting this [link](https://forms.gle/AXcDYzZ7EEqMjjw4A) (https://forms.gle/AXcDYzZ7EEqMjjw4A), you can access our Macronutrient Assessment Form. This form is designed to gather essential information about you, which will enable me to create a personalized macronutrient breakdown tailored to your specific needs and goals. Whether you're aiming for weight loss, muscle gain, or overall well-being, this customized plan will be your roadmap to success. Take the first step towards a healthier you by filling out the form, and let's embark on this transformative journey together.

Recipes and Meal Ideas

Introduction: Healthy Eating Doesn't Mean Bland Food

One common misconception about healthy eating is that it equates to bland and uninspiring meals. In reality, embracing a nutritious lifestyle opens up a world of delicious possibilities. In this chapter, we'll explore a collection of 50 delightful recipes spanning breakfast, lunch, dinner, snacks, and desserts. Not only are these dishes packed with flavor, but we'll also provide a detailed macro breakdown for each recipe to help you maintain your dietary goals.

Breakfast

Avocado and Tomato Breakfast Burrito

Ingredients:

- 2 large eggs

- 1 whole-wheat tortilla

- 1/2 avocado, sliced

- 1/2 cup diced tomatoes

- Salt and pepper to taste

- Salsa for garnish (optional)

Directions:

1. In a bowl, beat the eggs and season with salt and pepper.

2. Heat a non-stick skillet over medium heat and add the beaten eggs. Scramble until cooked to your liking.

3. Warm the tortilla in the skillet or microwave for a few seconds.

4. Lay the scrambled eggs, avocado slices, and diced tomatoes in the center of the tortilla.

5. Fold in the sides and roll up the tortilla.

6. Serve with salsa if desired.

Macros per serving: Protein: 15g, Fat: 12g, Carbohydrates: 25g

Greek Yogurt Parfait

Ingredients:

- 1 cup Greek yogurt
- 1/2 cup mixed berries (strawberries, blueberries, raspberries)
- 1/4 cup granola
- Honey for drizzling (optional)

Directions:

1. In a glass or bowl, start with a layer of Greek yogurt.
2. Add a layer of mixed berries on top of the yogurt.
3. Sprinkle granola over the berries.
4. Repeat the layers until you fill your serving dish.
5. Drizzle with honey for extra sweetness if desired.

Macros per serving: Protein: 20g, Fat: 5g, Carbohydrates: 30g

Spinach and Mushroom Omelette

Ingredients:

- 2 large eggs

- 1/2 cup fresh spinach leaves

- 1/4 cup sliced mushrooms

- 2 tablespoons diced onion

- 1/4 cup shredded cheese (optional)

- Salt and pepper to taste

- Cooking spray or olive oil

Directions:

1. Heat a non-stick skillet over medium heat and add cooking spray or a small amount of olive oil.

2. Saute onions and mushrooms until they start to soften.

3. Add spinach leaves and cook until wilted.

4. In a bowl, beat the eggs and season with salt and pepper.

5. Pour the beaten eggs into the skillet over the vegetables.

6. Cook until the edges set, then lift the edges to allow uncooked eggs to flow underneath.

7. Sprinkle shredded cheese (if using) on one half of the omelet.

8. Fold the other half over the cheese and cook until the cheese melts and the omelet is fully set.

Macros per serving: Protein: 18g, Fat: 10g, Carbohydrates: 6g

Quinoa Breakfast Bowl with Berries

Ingredients:

- 1/2 cup cooked quinoa
- 1/2 cup mixed berries (strawberries, blueberries, raspberries)
- 2 tablespoons honey
- 1/4 cup Greek yogurt
- 1 tablespoon chopped nuts (e.g., almonds, walnuts)

Directions:

1. In a bowl, start with a layer of cooked quinoa.
2. Add a layer of mixed berries on top of the quinoa.
3. Drizzle with honey for sweetness.
4. Top with a dollop of Greek yogurt.
5. Sprinkle with chopped nuts for added crunch.

Macros per serving: Protein: 12g, Fat: 8g, Carbohydrates: 40g

Banana Nut Pancakes

Ingredients:

- 1 ripe banana, mashed
- 1 egg
- 1/4 cup rolled oats
- 1/4 cup chopped nuts (e.g., walnuts, almonds)
- 1/2 teaspoon baking powder
- 1/2 teaspoon cinnamon
- Cooking spray or olive oil

Directions:

1. In a bowl, combine mashed banana, egg, oats, chopped nuts, baking powder, and cinnamon.
2. Heat a non-stick skillet over medium heat and add cooking spray or a small amount of olive oil.
3. Pour small portions of the batter onto the skillet to make pancakes.
4. Cook until bubbles form on the surface, then flip and cook until golden brown on both sides.

Macros per serving: Protein: 10g, Fat: 6g, Carbohydrates: 35g

Lunch

Grilled Chicken Salad with Balsamic Vinaigrette

Ingredients:

- 4 oz grilled chicken breast
- 2 cups mixed greens (lettuce, spinach, arugula)
- 1/4 cup cherry tomatoes, halved
- 1/4 cup cucumber slices
- 2 tablespoons balsamic vinaigrette dressing

Directions:

1. Season the grilled chicken breast with salt and pepper.
2. Grill until cooked through and slightly charred.
3. Slice the grilled chicken into thin strips.
4. In a large bowl, combine the mixed greens, cherry tomatoes, and cucumber slices.
5. Top with grilled chicken strips.
6. Drizzle with balsamic vinaigrette dressing.

Macros per serving: Protein: 25g, Fat: 10g, Carbohydrates: 15g

Quinoa and Black Bean Stuffed Bell Peppers

Ingredients:

- 2 bell peppers, any color
- 1/2 cup cooked quinoa
- 1/2 cup canned black beans, drained and rinsed
- 1/4 cup corn kernels (fresh or frozen)
- 1/4 cup diced tomatoes
- 1/4 cup shredded cheese (optional)
- Taco seasoning (to taste)

Directions:

1. Preheat the oven to 375°F (190°C).
2. Cut the tops off the bell peppers and remove seeds and membranes.
3. In a bowl, mix quinoa, black beans, corn, diced tomatoes, and taco seasoning.
4. Stuff the bell peppers with the quinoa mixture.
5. Top with shredded cheese if desired.
6. Place the stuffed bell peppers in a baking dish and bake for 25-30 minutes or until the peppers are tender.

Macros per serving: Protein: 15g, Fat: 6g, Carbohydrates: 30g

Mediterranean Chickpea Wrap

Ingredients:

- 1 whole-wheat tortilla
- 1/2 cup canned chickpeas, drained and rinsed
- 2 tablespoons hummus
- 1/4 cup diced cucumber
- 1/4 cup diced tomatoes
- 1/4 cup sliced olives
- 2 tablespoons crumbled feta cheese
- Fresh parsley for garnish (optional)

Directions:

1. Warm the whole-wheat tortilla.
2. In a bowl, mix chickpeas, hummus, diced cucumber, diced tomatoes, and sliced olives.
3. Spread the chickpea mixture onto the tortilla.
4. Sprinkle with crumbled feta cheese and garnish with fresh parsley if desired.
5. Roll up the tortilla, and it's ready to eat.

Macros per serving: Protein: 20g, Fat: 12g, Carbohydrates: 35g

Salmon and Avocado Sushi Bowl

Ingredients:

- 4 oz grilled or baked salmon
- 1 cup cooked brown rice
- 1/2 avocado, sliced
- 1/4 cup cucumber slices
- 1/4 cup sliced carrots
- 1 sheet nori (seaweed), crumbled (optional)
- Soy sauce or low-sodium teriyaki sauce for drizzling

Directions:

1. Cook brown rice according to package instructions and let it cool.

2. Season salmon with your choice of seasoning (e.g., soy sauce, lemon, herbs) and grill or bake until cooked through.

3. In a bowl, layer cooked brown rice, grilled salmon, avocado slices, cucumber slices, and sliced carrots

Macros per serving: Protein: 22g, Fat: 15g, Carbohydrates: 35g

Veggie and Hummus Wrap

Ingredients:

- 1 whole-grain or whole-wheat tortilla
- 2 tablespoons hummus
- 1 cup mixed fresh vegetables (e.g., bell peppers, cucumbers, carrots, lettuce)
- 1/4 cup diced tomatoes
- 1/4 cup sliced olives (optional)
- Salt and pepper to taste

Directions:

1. Lay the tortilla flat on a clean surface.
2. Spread a layer of hummus evenly across the tortilla, leaving a small border around the edges.
3. Place the mixed vegetables, diced tomatoes, and sliced olives (if using) on top of the hummus.
4. Season with salt and pepper to taste.
5. Roll the tortilla tightly, folding in the sides as you go.
6. Slice the wrap in half diagonally and serve.

Macros per serving: Protein: 10g, Fat: 8g, Carbohydrates: 30g

Dinner

Baked Lemon Herb Tilapia

Ingredients:

- 4 tilapia fillets
- 2 tablespoons olive oil
- 2 cloves garlic, minced
- 1 lemon, juiced and zested
- 1 teaspoon dried oregano
- 1 teaspoon dried thyme
- Salt and pepper to taste
- Lemon wedges for garnish (optional)

Directions:

1. Preheat the oven to 375°F (190°C) and grease a baking dish.
2. Place the tilapia fillets in the baking dish.
3. In a small bowl, whisk together the olive oil, minced garlic, lemon juice, lemon zest, dried oregano, dried thyme, salt, and pepper.

4. Pour the lemon herb mixture over the tilapia fillets.

5. Bake in the preheated oven for about 15-20 minutes or until the fish flakes easily with a fork.

6. Garnish with lemon wedges if desired and serve.

Macros per serving: Protein: 30g, Fat: 8g, Carbohydrates: 5g

Spaghetti Squash with Tomato Basil Sauce

Ingredients:

- 1 medium spaghetti squash

- 2 cups tomato basil sauce (homemade or store-bought)

- Fresh basil leaves for garnish

- Grated Parmesan cheese (optional)

- Salt and pepper to taste

Directions:

1. Preheat the oven to 375°F (190°C).

2. Cut the spaghetti squash in half lengthwise and scoop out the seeds.

3. Place the squash halves, cut side down, on a baking sheet lined with parchment paper.

4. Bake for 30-40 minutes or until the squash is tender and the flesh can be easily scraped into "spaghetti" strands with a fork.

5. While the squash is baking, heat the tomato basil sauce in a saucepan over low heat.

6. Once the squash is done, use a fork to scrape the flesh into strands.

7. Serve the spaghetti squash with the heated tomato basil sauce on top.

8. Garnish with fresh basil leaves, grated Parmesan cheese (if desired), and season with salt and pepper to taste.

Macros per serving: Protein: 12g, Fat: 6g, Carbohydrates: 40g

Chicken and Vegetable Stir-Fry

Ingredients:

- 2 boneless, skinless chicken breasts, thinly sliced
- 2 tablespoons vegetable oil
- 1 red bell pepper, thinly sliced
- 1 yellow bell pepper, thinly sliced
- 1 cup broccoli florets
- 1 cup snow peas, trimmed
- 1/2 cup sliced carrots
- 2 cloves garlic, minced
- 1/4 cup low-sodium soy sauce
- 2 tablespoons hoisin sauce
- 1 teaspoon cornstarch
- Salt and pepper to taste
- Cooked brown rice or quinoa for serving

Directions:

1. In a small bowl, whisk together the soy sauce, hoisin sauce, and cornstarch. Set aside.

2. Heat 1 tablespoon of vegetable oil in a large skillet or wok over medium-high heat.

3. Add the sliced chicken and stir-fry until cooked through and no longer pink. Remove the chicken from the skillet and set aside.

4. In the same skillet, add the remaining 1 tablespoon of vegetable oil.

5. Add the minced garlic and stir-fry for about 30 seconds until fragrant.

6. Add the sliced bell peppers, broccoli, snow peas, and carrots to the skillet. Stir-fry for 3-4 minutes or until the vegetables are tender-crisp.

7. Return the cooked chicken to the skillet and pour the sauce mixture over the chicken and vegetables.

8. Stir-fry for an additional 2-3 minutes until the sauce thickens and coats the chicken and vegetables.

9. Season with salt and pepper to taste.

10. Serve the chicken and vegetable stir-fry over cooked brown rice or quinoa.

Macros per serving: Protein: 25g, Fat: 10g, Carbohydrates: 30g

Grilled Portobello Mushrooms with Quinoa

Ingredients:

- 4 large Portobello mushrooms, cleaned and stems removed
- 2 tablespoons olive oil
- 2 cloves garlic, minced
- 1/4 cup balsamic vinegar
- 2 cups cooked quinoa
- 1 cup cherry tomatoes, halved
- 1/4 cup fresh basil leaves, chopped
- Salt and pepper to taste
- Grated Parmesan cheese (optional)

Directions:

1. In a small bowl, whisk together the olive oil, minced garlic, and balsamic vinegar.
2. Brush the Portobello mushrooms with the balsamic mixture on both sides.
3. Preheat a grill or grill pan to medium-high heat.
4. Grill the Portobello mushrooms for 4-5 minutes per side or until they are tender and have grill marks.

5. While the mushrooms are grilling, in a large bowl, combine the cooked quinoa, halved cherry tomatoes, and chopped basil.

6. Season the quinoa mixture with salt and pepper to taste.

7. Once the Portobello mushrooms are done, slice them and serve them over the quinoa mixture.

8. If desired, sprinkle with grated Parmesan cheese before serving.

Macros per serving: Protein: 15g, Fat: 10g, Carbohydrates: 30g

Cauliflower Crust Margherita Pizza

Ingredients:

For the Cauliflower Crust:

- 1 medium cauliflower head, florets separated

- 1/4 cup grated Parmesan cheese

- 1/4 cup mozzarella cheese, shredded

- 1/2 teaspoon dried oregano

- 1/2 teaspoon garlic powder

- 1/4 teaspoon salt

- 1 egg, beaten

For the Toppings:

- 1/2 cup tomato sauce (low-sugar or homemade)

- 1 cup mozzarella cheese, shredded

- Fresh basil leaves

- Sliced tomatoes

- Salt and pepper to taste

Directions:

For the Cauliflower Crust:

1. Preheat your oven to 425°F (220°C) and line a baking sheet with parchment paper.

2. Place the cauliflower florets in a food processor and pulse until they resemble fine crumbs.

3. Transfer the cauliflower crumbs to a microwave-safe bowl and microwave on high for 4-5 minutes.

4. Allow the cauliflower to cool slightly, then place it in a clean kitchen towel and squeeze out as much moisture as possible.

5. In a mixing bowl, combine the cauliflower crumbs, grated Parmesan cheese, shredded mozzarella cheese, dried oregano, garlic powder, salt, and beaten egg.

6. Mix until all the ingredients are well combined.

For Assembling and Baking the Pizza:

1. Place the cauliflower mixture on the prepared baking sheet and shape it into a round pizza crust, about 1/4 inch thick.

2. Bake the cauliflower crust in the preheated oven for 15-20 minutes or until it's golden and holds together.

3. Remove the cauliflower crust from the oven and let it cool for a few minutes.

4. Spread the tomato sauce evenly over the cauliflower crust, leaving a small border around the edges.

5. Sprinkle the shredded mozzarella cheese over the tomato sauce.

6. Top with fresh basil leaves and sliced tomatoes.

7. Season with salt and pepper to taste.

8. Place the pizza back in the oven and bake for an additional 10-15 minutes or until the cheese is bubbly and slightly browned.

9. Once done, remove the cauliflower crust Margherita pizza from the oven, slice, and serve.

Macros per serving: Protein: 12g, Fat: 8g, Carbohydrates: 20g

Snacks

Greek Yogurt and Berry Smoothie

Ingredients:

- 1 cup Greek yogurt

- 1/2 cup mixed berries (e.g., strawberries, blueberries, raspberries)

- 1/2 banana

- 1/2 cup almond milk (or your preferred milk)

- 1 tablespoon honey (optional)

- Ice cubes (optional)

Directions:

1. Place the Greek yogurt, mixed berries, banana, almond milk, and honey (if using) in a blender.

2. Add a few ice cubes if you want a colder smoothie.

3. Blend until smooth and creamy.

4. Taste and adjust sweetness by adding more honey if desired.

5. Pour into a glass and enjoy your protein-packed berry smoothie!

Macros per serving: Protein: 15g, Fat: 3g, Carbohydrates: 25g

Hummus and Veggie Platter

Ingredients:

- 1/2 cup hummus
- Baby carrots
- Cherry tomatoes
- Cucumber slices
- Bell pepper strips (red, yellow, or green)
- Celery sticks
- Sliced radishes (optional)
- Olives (optional)
- Whole-grain crackers (optional)

Directions:

1. Arrange the hummus in the center of a serving platter.
2. Surround the hummus with an assortment of baby carrots, cherry tomatoes, cucumber slices, bell pepper strips, celery sticks, sliced radishes (if using), and olives (if using).
3. Add whole-grain crackers if you like.
4. Serve the veggie platter as a healthy snack or appetizer.

Macros per serving: Protein: 5g, Fat: 7g, Carbohydrates: 15g

Trail Mix with Nuts and Dried Fruit

Ingredients:

- 1/2 cup mixed nuts (almonds, cashews, walnuts)

- 1/4 cup dried cranberries

- 1/4 cup dried apricots, chopped

- 1/4 cup dark chocolate chips (optional)

- 1/4 cup pumpkin seeds (optional)

Directions:

1. In a bowl, combine the mixed nuts, dried cranberries, dried apricots, dark chocolate chips (if using), and pumpkin seeds (if using).

2. Toss everything together until well mixed.

3. Portion the trail mix into small snack-sized containers or resealable bags for easy, on-the-go snacking.

Macros per serving: Protein: 7g, Fat: 10g, Carbohydrates: 25g

Cottage Cheese with Pineapple

Ingredients:

- 1 cup low-fat cottage cheese
- 1/2 cup fresh pineapple chunks

Directions:

1. In a bowl, scoop out the cottage cheese.
2. Top it with fresh pineapple chunks.
3. Enjoy this simple and protein-packed snack.

Macros per serving: Protein: 15g, Fat: 3g, Carbohydrates: 20g

Roasted Chickpeas

Ingredients:

- 1 can (15 ounces) chickpeas (garbanzo beans), drained and rinsed
- 1 tablespoon olive oil
- 1 teaspoon paprika
- 1/2 teaspoon cumin
- 1/2 teaspoon garlic powder
- Salt and pepper to taste

Directions:

1. Preheat your oven to 400°F (200°C) and line a baking sheet with parchment paper.
2. In a bowl, combine the chickpeas, olive oil, paprika, cumin, garlic powder, salt, and pepper.
3. Toss until the chickpeas are well coated with the seasonings.
4. Spread the chickpeas in a single layer on the prepared baking sheet.
5. Roast in the preheated oven for 20-25 minutes or until the chickpeas are crispy and slightly golden brown.
6. Allow them to cool before enjoying your crunchy roasted chickpeas.

Macros per serving: Protein: 6g, Fat: 3g, Carbohydrates: 22g

Desserts

Chia Seed Pudding with Berries

Ingredients:

- 2 tablespoons chia seeds
- 1/2 cup almond milk (or your preferred milk)
- 1/2 teaspoon vanilla extract
- 1 tablespoon honey or maple syrup (optional)
- Mixed berries (e.g., strawberries, blueberries, raspberries) for topping

Directions:

1. In a bowl, combine the chia seeds, almond milk, vanilla extract, and honey or maple syrup (if using).
2. Stir well to mix all the ingredients.
3. Cover the bowl and refrigerate for at least 2 hours or overnight, allowing the chia seeds to absorb the liquid and thicken.

4. When ready to serve, top the chia seed pudding with mixed berries.

5. Enjoy this nutritious and satisfying dessert or snack.

Macros per serving: Protein: 10g, Fat: 8g, Carbohydrates: 25g

Dark Chocolate Avocado Mousse

Ingredients:

- 2 ripe avocados
- 1/4 cup unsweetened cocoa powder
- 1/4 cup honey or maple syrup
- 1 teaspoon vanilla extract
- 1/4 cup almond milk (or your preferred milk)
- Dark chocolate chips for garnish (optional)

Directions:

1. Cut the avocados in half, remove the pits, and scoop out the flesh into a blender.

2. Add the unsweetened cocoa powder, honey or maple syrup, vanilla extract, and almond milk to the blender.

3. Blend until smooth and creamy.

4. Taste and adjust sweetness if needed by adding more honey or maple syrup.

5. Transfer the mousse to serving dishes and garnish with dark chocolate chips if desired.

6. Chill for a couple of hours before serving your rich and creamy dark chocolate avocado mousse.

Macros per serving: Protein: 5g, Fat: 12g, Carbohydrates: 20g

Baked Apple with Cinnamon and Almonds

Ingredients:

- 2 apples (e.g., Granny Smith or Honeycrisp)

- 1/4 cup chopped almonds

- 1 teaspoon ground cinnamon

- 1 tablespoon honey (optional)

- 1 tablespoon lemon juice

Directions:

1. Preheat your oven to 350°F (175°C).

2. Core the apples and remove the seeds, leaving the bottoms intact.

3. In a bowl, combine the chopped almonds, ground cinnamon, and honey (if using).

4. Stuff the center of each apple with the almond mixture.

5. Place the stuffed apples in a baking dish and drizzle them with lemon juice.

6. Bake in the preheated oven for 25-30 minutes or until the apples are tender.

7. Serve your baked apples warm, optionally topped with a dollop of Greek yogurt for added protein.

Macros per serving: Protein: 4g, Fat: 5g, Carbohydrates: 30g

Frozen Banana and Peanut Butter Bites

Ingredients:

- 2 ripe bananas
- 1/4 cup natural peanut butter
- Dark chocolate chips (optional)

Directions:

1. Peel the bananas and slice them into rounds, about 1/2 inch thick.

2. Spread a small amount of peanut butter on half of the banana slices.

3. Top with the remaining banana slices to create little banana "sandwiches."

4. Optional: Melt dark chocolate chips and drizzle over the banana bites for extra flavor.

5. Place the banana bites on a baking sheet lined with parchment paper.

6. Freeze for at least 2 hours until the bites are firm.

7. Enjoy your frozen banana and peanut butter bites as a tasty frozen treat!

Macros per serving: Protein: 8g, Fat: 6g, Carbohydrates: 25g

Mixed Berry Sorbet

Ingredients:

- 2 cups mixed berries (e.g., strawberries, blueberries, raspberries)
- 1/4 cup honey or maple syrup (adjust to taste)
- 1 tablespoon lemon juice
- 1/4 cup water

Directions:

1. Place the mixed berries, honey or maple syrup, lemon juice, and water in a blender.
2. Blend until smooth.
3. Taste and adjust sweetness by adding more honey or maple syrup if needed.
4. Pour the berry mixture into an ice cream maker and churn according to the manufacturer's instructions until it reaches a sorbet-like consistency.
5. Alternatively, if you don't have an ice cream maker, pour the mixture into a shallow container.
6. Freeze the container for about 2 hours, then stir the mixture with a fork to break up any ice crystals.

7. Return it to the freezer and repeat the stirring process every 30 minutes for about 2-3 hours or until the sorbet is firm.

8. Scoop and serve your refreshing mixed berry sorbet!

Enjoy this delightful, low-fat dessert with a burst of berry flavor and minimal added sugars.

Macros per serving: Protein: 2g, Fat: 0g, Carbohydrates: 30g

These recipes prove that healthy eating can be both delicious and satisfying while providing the essential macronutrients your body needs to thrive. Enjoy experimenting with these flavorful dishes on your journey to a healthier lifestyle.

Supplements and Macronutrients

In our quest for optimal nutrition and overall well-being, we often turn to supplements as a means to bridge the gap between our dietary choices and our macronutrient goals. This chapter explores the essential role of supplements in meeting macronutrient goals, offers considerations for their use, delves into the importance of safety and quality, and guides you on how to supplement wisely for a balanced and healthy life.

Role of Supplements in Meeting Macronutrient Goals

Bridging Nutritional Gaps

In an ideal world, we would obtain all our macronutrients—protein, fats, and carbohydrates—from whole foods. However, the reality is that our diets may fall short of meeting our nutritional needs due to various factors, including dietary restrictions, food availability, and individual preferences. Supplements can step in as valuable allies in filling these nutritional gaps.

Achieving Specific Goals

Supplements are particularly beneficial when striving to achieve specific macronutrient goals, such as:

1. **Protein:** Protein supplements like whey, casein, or plant-based protein powders can help individuals meet their daily protein intake requirements, especially for athletes and those aiming to build muscle.

2. **Fats:** Omega-3 fatty acid supplements can be valuable for individuals with limited access to fatty fish, aiding in cardiovascular health and brain function.

3. **Carbohydrates:** Carbohydrate supplements, like maltodextrin or dextrose, can benefit endurance athletes who need quick energy sources during intense workouts or competitions.

Considerations for Macronutrient Supplements

Dietary Diversity

Supplements should complement, not replace, a balanced diet. It's crucial to prioritize whole foods, as they provide essential micronutrients, fiber, and phytonutrients that supplements cannot fully replicate. Supplements are most effective when used strategically to meet specific macronutrient goals.

Individual Needs

Your macronutrient requirements are unique to your age, gender, activity level, and health goals. Consider consulting a healthcare professional or registered dietitian to determine the right supplements and dosages that align with your individual needs.

Timing and Use

The timing of macronutrient supplements matters. For example, protein supplements are often consumed post-workout to aid in muscle recovery, while carbohydrate supplements can be ingested before or during prolonged exercise for energy.

Safety and Quality of Supplements

Regulatory Oversight

Supplement quality varies widely, so it's essential to choose products from reputable manufacturers. Look for supplements that have undergone third-party testing for safety and potency. In the United States, the FDA regulates supplements, but they are not subject to the same rigorous testing as pharmaceuticals.

Potential Risks

Supplement misuse can carry risks. Excessive protein intake, for instance, may strain the kidneys. Additionally, fat-soluble vitamins (A, D, E, K) can accumulate in the body and cause toxicity if taken in excess. Always follow recommended dosages and guidelines.

Supplementing Wisely

Assess Your Diet

Before turning to supplements, evaluate your dietary habits. Aim to obtain as many macronutrients as possible from whole foods. Adjust your meal planning and food choices to meet your macronutrient goals naturally.

Seek Professional Guidance

Consulting a registered dietitian or healthcare provider is wise when considering macronutrient supplements. They can provide personalized recommendations based on your health status, dietary preferences, and goals.

Monitor Progress

Supplements should enhance your overall nutrition. Regularly assess your macronutrient intake and adjust your supplement regimen as your goals evolve. Remember that supplementing is a tool within a broader dietary strategy.

In conclusion, supplements can be valuable allies in helping you meet your macronutrient goals and achieve optimal nutrition. However, their role should be strategic and supportive of a balanced diet rich in whole foods. Prioritize safety, quality, and professional guidance when considering macronutrient supplements, and remember that your dietary choices lay the foundation for a healthier life.

Tracking Macronutrients

In the pursuit of a healthier and more balanced diet, tracking macronutrients has emerged as a powerful tool. This chapter delves into the practical aspects of tracking your macronutrient intake, including the use of apps and tools, the benefits of maintaining a macronutrient diary, tracking your progress, and strategies for staying consistent with your tracking efforts.

Using Apps and Tools for Tracking

1. Mobile Apps: Numerous mobile apps are designed to simplify macronutrient tracking. These apps often come with extensive databases of food items, making it easy to log your meals and calculate macronutrient intake. Some popular options include MyFitnessPal, Cronometer, and Lose It!

2. Online Tools: Web-based macronutrient calculators and tracking platforms provide a user-friendly interface for recording your dietary intake. They often offer features like barcode scanning, recipe creation, and meal planning.

3. **Wearable Devices:** Some fitness trackers and smartwatches can track your daily calorie and macronutrient expenditure, giving you real-time feedback on your nutritional goals.

4. **Food Scales:** For precise measurements of portion sizes, a digital food scale can be a valuable tool. It helps you accurately gauge your macronutrient intake, especially for foods without nutrition labels.

Benefits of Keeping a Macronutrient Diary

1. **Awareness:** Tracking macronutrients cultivates awareness of what you eat. It highlights your dietary patterns and habits, enabling you to identify areas for improvement.

2. **Goal Alignment:** A macronutrient diary allows you to align your dietary choices with specific goals. Whether you're aiming for weight loss, muscle gain, or improved energy levels, tracking helps you tailor your nutrition.

3. **Portion Control:** It assists in portion control by providing insights into serving sizes. This awareness can prevent overeating and support weight management.

4. Adjustment: Tracking facilitates adjustments. If your macronutrient intake isn't meeting your goals, you can modify your diet accordingly.

Tracking Your Progress

1. **Regular Assessments:** Periodically review your macronutrient diary to evaluate your progress. Are you consistently meeting your targets? Are you making adjustments based on your goals?

2. **Body Measurements:** Consider taking body measurements or tracking changes in weight, body composition, and energy levels to assess the impact of your macronutrient intake on your overall health.

3. **Performance Metrics:** For athletes or fitness enthusiasts, monitor performance metrics like strength gains, endurance, and recovery. Macronutrient tracking can influence athletic performance.

Staying Consistent with Tracking

1. **Set Realistic Goals:** Establish achievable macronutrient goals. Unrealistic targets can lead to frustration and may not be sustainable.

2. Plan Ahead: Prepare your meals and snacks in advance, and log them into your tracking tool. Planning makes it easier to stay within your macronutrient limits.

3. Stay Organized: Keep a record of your favorite recipes and meals. This simplifies tracking when you consume these items regularly.

4. Be Patient: Tracking macronutrients can be challenging initially, but it becomes more intuitive with practice. Be patient with yourself as you learn the ropes.

5. Seek Support: Share your tracking journey with a friend or a support group. Accountability can boost your consistency.

6. Flexibility: While consistency is key, remember that perfection isn't necessary. Occasional deviations from your macronutrient targets won't derail your progress.

7. Celebrate Milestones: Acknowledge and celebrate your achievements. Whether it's hitting a weight loss milestone or consistently meeting your protein intake, recognizing your successes can help maintain motivation.

In conclusion, tracking macronutrients is a valuable tool for optimizing your nutrition and achieving your dietary goals. Utilizing apps and tools, understanding the benefits of a macronutrient diary, regularly assessing your progress, and staying consistent with tracking efforts can empower you to take control of your diet and work towards a healthier and more balanced lifestyle.

Common Challenges and Solutions

In the journey towards mastering macronutrient management, it's essential to navigate common challenges effectively. This chapter will provide practical solutions for addressing challenges such as macronutrient management difficulties, overcoming plateaus, handling social and environmental pressures, and staying committed to nutritional goals.

Addressing Common Challenges in Macronutrient Management

- ❖ **Challenge:** Calculating macronutrient intake accurately can be daunting, leading to over or underestimating.

- ❖ **Solution:** Invest in a food scale for precise measurements. Use mobile apps or online tools to simplify tracking. Consult a registered dietitian for guidance in setting accurate macronutrient goals.

- **Challenge:** Finding the right balance of macronutrients can be challenging, especially when dietary preferences and restrictions come into play.

- **Solution:** Explore different dietary approaches like Mediterranean, plant-based, or low-carb to find what suits you best. Customize your macronutrient ratios based on your dietary needs and preferences while still meeting your goals.

Overcoming Plateaus

- **Challenge:** Hitting a weight loss or muscle gain plateau can be discouraging.

- **Solution:** Periodically adjust your macronutrient goals to match your changing needs. Incorporate variety into your workouts to challenge your body. Ensure you're getting enough sleep and managing stress, as these factors can impact progress.

- **Challenge:** Feeling stuck in a routine and losing motivation.

- **Solution:** Set short-term goals and rewards to keep motivation high. Join a fitness class or hire a trainer for fresh perspectives. Engage in mindful eating practices to rekindle your passion for nutritious meals.

Handling Social and Environmental Pressures

- **Challenge:** Social gatherings and events often involve tempting, unhealthy foods.

- **Solution:** Plan ahead by eating a balanced meal or snack before attending. Offer to bring a nutritious dish to share. Politely decline foods that don't align with your goals. Remember, it's okay to indulge occasionally in moderation.

- **Challenge:** Peer pressure and well-meaning family members may push you to abandon your dietary goals.

- **Solution:** Communicate your goals with loved ones, so they understand your commitment. Engage in open conversations about your nutritional choices, educating them about your reasons. Seek their support and involvement in your journey.

Staying Committed to Your Nutritional Goals

- **Challenge:** Life's demands, stress, and busy schedules can disrupt your commitment.

Common Challenges and Solutions

- **Solution:** Prioritize self-care by managing stress through practices like meditation or yoga. Meal prep to ensure healthy options are readily available. Maintain a flexible approach, allowing for occasional adjustments in your routine.

- **Challenge:** Loss of motivation over time.

- **Solution:** Regularly revisit your goals and remind yourself why you started. Join support groups or forums to connect with others on similar journeys. Celebrate small victories and milestones to maintain motivation.

By addressing these common challenges and implementing practical solutions, you can overcome obstacles in macronutrient management effectively. Remember that the journey to better nutrition is a lifelong commitment. The ability to adapt and persevere is key to your success as you aim for optimal health and well-being.

Achieving Long-Term Nutritional Success

In your quest for long-term nutritional success, it's essential to adopt sustainable practices, maintain a healthy macronutrient balance, integrate valuable tips for overall well-being, and embrace your journey to nutritional mastery. This chapter provides a comprehensive guide to equip you with the knowledge and tools needed to embark on this empowering path.

Sustainable Nutrition Practices

1. Mindful Eating: Cultivate mindful eating habits by savoring each bite, paying attention to hunger cues, and enjoying your meals without distractions. This fosters a healthier relationship with food.

2. Whole Foods Focus: Base your diet on whole, minimally processed foods. These nutrient-dense choices provide essential vitamins, minerals, and fiber, promoting optimal health.

3. Gradual Changes: Make dietary changes gradually to allow for adjustment. This approach makes it easier to adopt new habits that stick.

4. Balanced and Varied Diet: Incorporate a variety of foods into your diet to ensure a wide range of nutrients. Strive for balance in your macronutrient intake, adjusting based on your individual goals and preferences.

Maintaining a Healthy Macronutrient Balance

1. Protein: Continue to prioritize protein intake to support muscle maintenance and overall health. Aim for lean sources like lean beef, poultry, fish, tofu, and legumes.

2. Fats: Choose healthy fats such as avocados, nuts, seeds, and olive oil. These fats support brain function, hormone production, and overall well-being.

3. Carbohydrates: Focus on complex carbohydrates from whole grains, fruits, vegetables, and legumes. These provide sustained energy and essential nutrients.

4. **Monitoring and Adjusting:** Regularly assess your macronutrient intake to ensure it aligns with your goals. Be flexible in making adjustments as needed based on your progress.

Tips for Long-Term Nutritional Wellness

1. **Hydration:** Stay adequately hydrated by consuming plenty of water throughout the day. Proper hydration supports digestion, metabolism, and overall health.

2. **Portion Control:** Maintain portion control by using smaller plates, measuring portions, and being mindful of portion sizes. This practice prevents overeating and supports weight management.

3. **Meal Planning:** Plan your meals and snacks in advance to ensure you have access to nutritious options when hunger strikes. This reduces the temptation of unhealthy choices.

4. **Regular Physical Activity:** Complement your nutrition with regular physical activity. Incorporate a variety of exercises you enjoy to stay motivated and maintain a healthy lifestyle.

5. **Sleep and Stress Management:** Prioritize sleep and manage stress through relaxation techniques, meditation, or yoga.

These practices have a profound impact on your overall well-being and nutritional success.

Your Journey to Nutritional Mastery

1. Set Realistic Goals: Establish achievable nutritional goals that align with your values and priorities. Break larger goals into smaller, manageable steps.

2. Learn and Adapt: Stay open to learning about nutrition, new foods, and cooking methods. Be willing to adapt as your nutritional knowledge grows.

3. Seek Support: Engage with a supportive community or seek guidance from a registered dietitian or healthcare professional when facing challenges or uncertainties.

4. Celebrate Achievements: Acknowledge your successes along the way. Celebrate milestones, both big and small, to maintain motivation and enthusiasm for your journey.

5. Embrace Resilience: Understand that setbacks are a part of any journey. Embrace resilience and use setbacks as opportunities to learn and grow.

In your pursuit of long-term nutritional success, remember that this journey is a marathon, not a sprint. Sustainable practices, a balanced macronutrient approach, valuable tips for overall well-being, and the embrace of your unique journey to nutritional mastery will empower you to thrive and maintain optimal health for years to come.

Embrace Nutritional Mastery for a Lifetime of Wellness

As we conclude our journey through "Mastering Macronutrients: A Guide to Optimal Nutrition," let's take a moment to recap the key takeaways.

Throughout this guide, we've explored the fundamental role of macronutrients—protein, fats, and carbohydrates—in our daily lives. We've learned how to assess our unique nutritional needs, set realistic goals, and navigate the challenges that may arise along the way.

Recap of Key Takeaways

1. **Understanding Macronutrients:** We've delved into the significance of each macronutrient and how they contribute to our health and well-being. Protein for strength, fats for brain

function, and carbohydrates for sustained energy.

2. **Balancing Act:** Achieving a balanced macronutrient intake is key. Customizing your ratios based on your goals and preferences ensures your diet aligns with your unique needs.

3. **Tracking and Consistency:** The use of tools, apps, and diaries for tracking is a powerful strategy. Regular assessment and consistency in your approach support long-term success.

4. **Challenges and Solutions:** We've explored common obstacles, such as plateaus and social pressures, and provided practical solutions to overcome them. Remember, you have the tools to face any challenge head-on.

Encouragement for Continued Nutritional Success

Your journey to nutritional mastery is a lifelong endeavor. Embrace it with the confidence that you are equipped with knowledge, skills, and a deep understanding of the significance of macronutrients in your life.

You hold the power to shape your nutritional destiny. Whether your goal is to maintain optimal health, lose weight, build

Embrace Nutritional Mastery for a Lifetime of Wellness

muscle, or simply feel your best, know that each step you take contributes to your overall wellness.

In the face of challenges and setbacks, remain resilient. Your commitment to lifelong nutritional success is a testament to your dedication to a healthier, happier you. Celebrate every achievement, big or small, and use each experience as an opportunity to learn and grow.

Remember that nutritional mastery is not about perfection but about progress. It's about making choices that align with your goals while still allowing room for enjoyment and flexibility. With each meal, each choice, and each day, you have the chance to reaffirm your commitment to your health and well-being.

As you close the chapter on this guide, carry with you the knowledge that mastering macronutrients is a dynamic and empowering journey—a journey that can lead to a lifetime of wellness, vitality, and fulfillment. Continue to nourish your body, nurture your spirit, and savor the joys of a healthy and balanced life.

Glossary

BMR (Basal Metabolic Rate): The number of calories your body needs to maintain basic functions at rest, such as breathing and circulation.

Carbohydrates: A macronutrient that provides the body's primary source of energy. It includes sugars, starches, and fibers found in foods like fruits, grains, and vegetables.

Fats: A macronutrient that serves as an energy source, aids in nutrient absorption, and supports various cellular functions. Includes healthy fats like monounsaturated and polyunsaturated fats.

Lean Proteins: Protein sources that are low in fat content, such as skinless poultry, lean cuts of meat, fish, and plant-based proteins like tofu and legumes.

Macronutrient Ratio: The proportion of macronutrients (protein, fats, and carbohydrates) in your diet. It can vary based on individual goals and dietary preferences.

Macronutrients: Essential nutrients required by the body in large quantities for energy and various physiological functions. The three primary macronutrients are protein, fats, and carbohydrates.

Mindful Eating: A practice of paying full attention to the eating experience, including the taste, texture, and satisfaction derived from food, to promote healthier eating habits.

Nutrient Density: A measure of how many essential nutrients a food contains relative to the number of calories it provides. Foods high in nutrient density offer more nutrients per calorie.

Nutrient-Dense Foods: Foods that provide a high concentration of essential nutrients (vitamins, minerals, and antioxidants) relative to their calorie content.

Plateau: A point in your progress where you no longer see significant changes or improvements, often experienced in weight loss or fitness goals.

Portion Control: The practice of managing the amount of food you consume in one sitting to prevent overeating and maintain a healthy diet.

Protein: A macronutrient essential for growth, tissue repair, and various bodily functions. Composed of amino acids, it's crucial for muscle development and overall health.

Resilience: The ability to bounce back from setbacks and challenges, a valuable trait in maintaining long-term nutritional success.

Sustainable Nutrition: Dietary practices that are environmentally friendly and can be maintained over the long term without harm to the planet or your health.

Whole Foods: Unprocessed or minimally processed foods that are close to their natural state and rich in nutrients. Examples include fruits, vegetables, whole grains, and lean proteins.

Whole Grains: Grains that contain the entire grain kernel, including the bran, germ, and endosperm. Examples include brown rice, whole wheat, and oats.

Made in the USA
Las Vegas, NV
18 January 2024